Florida Ghosts

SWEETWATER
PRESS

Florida Ghosts

Produced by Cliff Road Books

ISBN-13: 978-1-58173-520-8
ISBN-10: 1-58173-520-0

Book design by Pat Covert

Printed in the United States of America

Florida Ghosts

they are among us

Lynne L. Hall

SWEETWATER
PRESS

Table of Contents

They Are Among Us

They Are Among Us

I won't lie to you. I'm a skeptic. I mean, like everyone else, I grew up shivering delightedly to ghost stories. But for the most part, I believed my mama when she told me, "There're no such things as ghosts."

Later on, I spent a lot of time examining the world around me and trying to fit it all into one mold or the other. Religion? Or science? The great debate. One entirely spiritual, based on faith. The other, entirely logical, based on scientific evidence.

For many years, I fell solidly on the science side. It was that scientific evidence thing that got me. So, I spent a lot of time and effort ignoring the things that didn't fit my mold, chalking them up to coincidence or serendipity.

But years bring wisdom, and, if you're lucky, they open your heart and mind. I was lucky. I had an experience with the spiritual realm, a realm we can't see or touch, but one we know in our hearts exists.

It happened days after the death of Oleta—a woman who was dear to me, a woman who'd parented me as much, if not more, than my own parents. In the performance of my duties as a professional firefighter, I was about to go into a burning house. At the moment I crawled over the threshold, I heard Oleta's voice in my head: "Be careful, Lynne." In that moment I knew she was there, watching over me.

That experience brought a realization that, yes, there's scientific evidence for some things. But there're many other things that simply can't be explained by science, things that can only be known in your own heart. I found there was a place for both realms—that the spiritual could exist side by side with the logical.

Still, when it came to actual ghosts, ones that you have no connection to, that appeared and disappeared and made strange noises, I remained skeptical. So, I approached this project with a sense of fun, searching out stories that would be fun to tell and entertaining to read.

I found them, I think, but I also found something else. I found a collection of stories with common threads. In each story, there was a strong connection between the spirits and the places they were haunting. And there was something in their lives that, in death, seems to keep them bound to this world. Perhaps the death was a violent or sudden one. Or perhaps there was a loss of a great love. Whatever the reason, they're here. And they've made themselves known. They've been seen. They've been heard. And they can't be explained away by science.

It's enough to make a skeptic wonder if, indeed, they are among us.

Lynne L. Hall

The Lady with the Lantern

The Lady with the Lantern

Welcome to the Matanzas Hotel, Mr. Elliot," said the hotel's proprietress, as she turned the registry book for him to sign. "Are you here for business or pleasure?"

"A little of both, ma'am. A little of both," he replied.

Elliot couldn't help noticing that the innkeeper, a widow he'd heard, was a beautiful woman. Unlike many of the women he'd met lately, she wore her thick, dark hair long and her face was almost devoid of makeup. He so disliked the short hair, dark eyes, and red lips of those "flappers." Women who cut their hair and wore all that paint were women of questionable morals, Elliot thought. They were women who smoked cigarettes, drank whiskey, and, now that whiskey was prohibited, frequented speakeasies. Obviously, the widow here was a much finer woman.

The woman in question smiled at her new customer and handed him a key to a room at the back of the inn on the end furthest from the bay. As he hefted his valise and strode out of the lobby, she turned the registry around and examined his signature, a knowing smile on her face.

"More business than pleasure, eh, Mr. N. Elliot?" she mumbled to herself. Stepping from around the desk, she wandered out the front door. On the veranda, she hugged herself and took a quick look around the grounds of the hotel, solely hers since the death of her husband a year ago.

She had to admit, she loved the place. She loved the shady, bougainvillaea-framed veranda and the stately, Mediterranean-style building with its elegant interior. She loved the tropical scent that wafted to her from the hotel gardens and the silky feel of the salt-laden air on her skin. And she loved the fact that it was hers and hers alone. Not that she hadn't cared for her husband; she had. But he'd been so much older. She married him mostly for what he could give her, thinking she could stifle her youthful spirit and be happy with being mistress of the grand hotel. But, oh, he had been such an old Mrs. Grundy, always going on about the evils of alcohol and the moral depravity of the women who cut their hair and wore paint on their faces.

Her husband's idea of fun had been sedate walks around the grounds, topped off by a rousing game of mahjong with some of his old cronies in the hotel lobby. A night out on the town, of course, never included dancing or even a show. They maybe went to dinner at a local restaurant, and then she was all tucked into beddie-bye—alone—before 10 p.m. Holy moley! Things had been pretty boring around here.

She gazed across Matanzas Bay and smiled. Not anymore, she thought. Never again would she feel the overwhelming ennui that had gripped her in those days. Not since she'd met Bill and his friends. Since meeting the dark-haired, blue-eyed Bill six months ago, she'd felt a constant tingle of excitement that she'd never experienced before, a surprising self-awareness that kept her senses humming at a sometimes alarming pace.

No doubt about it, she was carrying a hot torch for the man. He was a dashing sea captain with dreamboat eyes and a heart as big as Matanzas Bay. Always fair with anyone he worked with, he had gained a reputation as the real McCoy in his business dealings. And, she almost giggled out loud, his mustache tickled when he kissed her. Since he'd stepped into her life, her days had become positively thrilling—and, by golly, quite profitable! Darn it. Because of her new guest, she wouldn't get to see him for another two weeks!

Thanks to the arrival of Mr. N. Elliot, she fumed, Bill and his fellow rum runners would have to bypass their stop at Matanzas Hotel. And she'd lose out on seeing Bill and on a lot of moola. She had everything ready. The back room of the hotel was set up for guests, and all the locals who were savvy had been notified that the party would be on tomorrow night. There was to be music and dancing and fun. And hooch. Bill always had the best Canadian and Irish whiskey and premium rum from the islands. He had promised some real French Champagne in this shipment—just for her.

The Champagne, he said, was to toast her—to celebrate their love and their success. Her hotel had become the hub of liquor smuggling, and they were both making a pretty penny off of it. So what if it was against the law? It was a stupid law. Who were these people who thought they had the right to tell her or anyone else that they couldn't have a drink or two when they wanted it?

She didn't feel the least bit guilty. In fact, she knew

deep in her soul that when she was old and gray, rocking her last days away here on the veranda, these were the days she'd most cherish, the ones she'd prattle on about to anyone who'd listen.

It didn't matter to her that she'd been called in for questioning about the smuggling activity in St. Augustine. They had questioned her endlessly, but she'd never given up anything to the Feds. And she never would. Why would she even consider letting her life slip back into a boring day-to-day existence with nothing to look forward to? She loved the excitement of it all—the tingling anticipation of another shipment arrival, the flash of heat brought on by the thought of Bill's arms around her.

They had nothing on her and they knew it. They just wanted to scare her. So she did her best to keep up appearances. It's why she hadn't cut her hair and why she never wore a lot of makeup. Her demure look and manner, accompanied by a flutter of her long, dark lashes, she knew, often convinced the G-men that she was just the victim of vicious rumors. Huh, she thought, they don't scare me. They're just a bunch of pussy cats if you play 'em right. And she was going to play them just right.

Well, can't keep sitting here, she thought. Plenty to do before tonight. She'd have to post the secret warning to her anticipated guests that they shouldn't show up tomorrow night. And there was still the marketing to do. Sighing, she rose from the veranda railing and started walking toward town.

It was well past midnight, and Mr. N. Elliot was out and about, walking lightly along the hotel path to the bay, trying to keep his footsteps from crunching and giving him away. He knew the rumors—that the Matanzas Hotel was the hub of smuggling here in St. Augustine, and that the good widow ran a speakeasy in a back room.

Yeah, he'd heard the rumors, but after meeting the modest widow, he found them hard to believe. He could no more see her touching illegal rum to her lips than he could see himself breaking a law. And that just wasn't going to happen. One thing he did know, however: there was a shipment due in to Matanzas Bay tonight and he planned to catch the brigands and bring them to justice.

Reaching the bay, his eyes scoured the water for anything untoward. Nothing. Moonlight shimmered on the placid bay waters, and for a moment he found himself enjoying the feel of the warm night air on his skin. For the merest split second, a desire hit him, a desire for dark eyes looking into his and the tickle of sweet breath caressing his neck.

Shaking it off, he strained his eyes to make out the silhouette of any boat that might be trying to sneak in under the meager light. But even his eagle eyes could discern nothing out of the way.

He turned west and started walking, skirting the bay and keeping his eyes and ears trained on the water. If they were here, he'd catch them, he knew. The information the Bureau had on St. Augustine was solid. Rum running was going on here and lots of it. Gallons of illegal liquor were docking here and finding their way into the country's interior. That's why he'd chosen the town for his trip. Nothing wrong, he smiled, with a little working vacation.

After he'd walked at least a mile, he turned and looked back toward the hotel. A light caught his eye. Someone was up high, waving a lantern of some sort. Waving it back and forth. Glancing back out to the waters, he knew its gleam would be visible way out at the mouth of the bay. He knew without a doubt that it was a signal for the smugglers to stay away. Chagrined, he realized they knew he was here. Jeepers. He'd traded in his department-issue suit for casual trousers and a pullover shirt, clothes he never wore unless working undercover. He looked like a typical tourist, didn't he? What could have gone wrong?

Well, he'd get nothing done here, he thought. Might as well move on—further south, perhaps. As he started walking dejectedly back to the hotel, he strained his eyes to see which roof the signal was coming from, but he was too far away. Could be any roof. Could be the roof of the Matanzas, but he couldn't prove it. And he couldn't believe it, either. The widow was too genteel. Her hotel too elegant. Why would she get herself involved in something illegal? Those dark, guileless eyes. That halo of ebony hair. A silky voice that made his stomach flutter. He just didn't believe it. Hmmm, maybe he should hang around awhile? No, he decided, duty calls.

Back at the Matanzas Hotel, the widow handed in her lantern and climbed back into the hotel from a window that looked out over the roof. She smiled at her assistant, Clara, and nodded. The deed was done. She'd watched Mr. N. Elliot, and had seen him walk around the bay. She had watched him as he paused momentarily, as if a bit wistful, then slowly moved on.

When he'd gotten far enough away, she'd climbed out onto the roof and with her lantern, she'd warned Bill and all the other smugglers out there that it wasn't safe to come in. She knew they'd simply leave the bay and move on up the coast, selling their wares further north, returning to St. Augustine in two weeks time. She'd sure have to figure out a way of getting rid of Mr. Elliot by then.

She needn't have worried. Early the next morning, Mr. N. Elliot presented to the front desk, valise in hand, and informed her that he was checking out.

"Oh," she said. "I hope there was nothing wrong with the accommodations," she said.

"Not at all," he replied with a smile. "It seems that my business here did not work out. I'm going to have to move on."

"Oh? And which way are you headed?"

"Further south, I guess. Maybe on down to the Keys. I've heard business is hopping down there."

The widow flashed him a big smile that made his heart lurch. "Oh, yes, Mr. Elliot. It really is hopping down there." She handed him his receipt. "You have a good trip, now."

Two weeks later, Mr. N. Elliot strode into the Chicago branch of the FBI. He was tanned, but the relaxation you'd expect from a man just returning from a Florida vacation wasn't there. He was strung tight. Not that it was a surprise to his coworkers. He was well-known for his devotion to duty and they knew that, although he had protested he was only going on vacation, he'd had business in mind. They knew, too, that he'd failed.

"So, Chief," braved a wet-behind-the-ears feebie. "Guess things didn't pan out in St. Augustine."

Mr. N. Elliot caught the guy in his blue-steel gaze and held him there long enough to make him squirm. "No, Johnson. They didn't. The smugglers got warned off at the last minute. But we'll get 'em next time. Now get off your butt and get busy. There're people breaking the law out there."

The tale of the Lady with the Lantern is a well-known story in St. Augustine, mainly because the widow is still making her presence known. Her beloved Matanzas Hotel, one of the first buildings constructed after a fire destroyed six city blocks in 1914, is now the Casablanca Inn. As she wanders the halls, she's no doubt proud of how things have turned out. Listed on the National Register of Historic Places, her graceful Mediterranean revival house is considered one of the ten best inns in the Southeast.

That's not what makes it so interesting, however. The interesting part is the fact that periodically, late at night, a lantern can be seen waving upon the roof of the inn. The phenomenon has been reported by the guests of surrounding hotels, who noticed a light coming through their windows. Thinking it was the lighthouse on Anastasia Island, they peeked out of the curtains to see a swinging light on the roof of the Casablanca Inn.

Sailors out in the bay also have reported seeing a light swinging from the inn's roof on many a dark night. Many of them also report seeing a dark figure holding the light and waving it back and forth.

In addition to these sightings, there have been reports that the widow has appeared inside her beloved inn. Guests report catching a fleeting glimpse of something or someone moving in hallways and stairways and incidences of items missing from their rooms, only to reappear in strange places later.

The present owners of the Casablanca Inn say they

discovered the story of the widow when they were doing some remodeling. They've declined to name her in deference to her descendants who still live in St. Augustine. No doubt they're delighted that, thanks to the widow and her swinging light, the inn is now included in St. Augustine's walking ghost tour. And thanks to the fact that folks love a good ghost story, the tour has become an excellent marketing tool.

No one knows why the widow still climbs the roof to swing her warning lantern. One story says that her rum runner lover was lost at sea when, after she'd warned him with her lantern, he'd stayed on in the waves of a coming hurricane. She never got over losing him, and that's why she continues to make her journey to the roof.

But we romantics discount that story. We think that no matter what became of the widow or of her seaman, the reason she still climbs out there on the roof with her lantern is that she's remembering. Remembering and reliving the best times of her life.

A Haunted Man

A Haunted Man

"Hey, Boss. That was Manny on the blower. It's done." That brought a smile to the face of Chicago's Public Enemy No. 1.

"Good. Did Bugsy make the party?"

"Don't know, yet. Manny said Machine Gun would give a yell with the dope later. He's laying low right now."

Al Capone nodded, and as his flunky left the room, he turned and looked out the window. The bright Florida sun shimmered on the Gulf waters. His smile returned. Here it was the middle of February and it was eighty degrees! Folks running around in shorts and swimsuits. In Chi-Town, he knew, it was thirty degrees. Streets full of palookas all bundled up in their overcoats. And if Manny had his dope straight, those streets were red with blood right now instead of white with snow.

A diabolical laugh escaped him. He knew he could trust McGurn and his hatchet men to get the job done. With a little luck, the coppers were measuring Bugs Moran and his goons for wooden kimonos right now.

Big Al Capone was all the way down in Florida when it all went down. Lighting a cigar and pouring himself a tumbler of his own bootleg whiskey, he laughed again. "Youse ain't got nothin' on me, G-man. I know nothin' from nothin'. Why, I was a thousand miles away, soaking up sunshine when Mr. Moran was soaking up all that lead!"

This was it, he exulted. It had been a bloody war, with wise guys gettin' whacked almost daily. He'd lost some good men. Yeah, the streets of Chicago had run bloody. He's paid a price himself, he thought, fingering the long scar along his face that had earned him that "Scarface" moniker he hated. But with Bugs Moran and his gang finally out of the way, Chi-Town was his.

Maybe he'd just run it from down here in sunny Florida. The weather was sure better. And Mae was fond of their little fourteen-room cabin here. Ironic, wasn't it, that he'd bought a mansion built from ol' Clarence Busch, the beer-brewing magnate. Yeah, and he was keen on Miami Beach, even if Miami Beach wasn't so keen on him. He'd show 'em. He was a good family man. He could put on the dog, just like them. They'd see.

He was going to show those Wall Street suckers a

thing or two about business, too. He was a millionaire. A self-made man. Just as good as any of those Miami swells that were tryin' to run him outta town. He'd show 'em all. See, diversity. That was the key. Prohibition was going to fail. He knew that, and that's why he'd been diversifying the business, so's he'd have a nice soft pillow for his fanny when that little gov'ment experiment hit the skids.

There was a knock on the door. "Machine Gun's on the horn."

Capone picked up the phone, "Spill."

"It's not good, Boss. Moran missed the party."

"Whaddya mean? How'd those guys miss him?"

"Ya got me. It all went down perfect. Bugsy fell for the scam like a sack of rocks. He had his gang at the warehouse waitin' for that truckload of hijacked hooch, just like we figured. Bet they were just gigglin' like little girls, thinking they was gettin' something over on us.

"Our guys came charging in dressed just like the coppers. They played it to the hilt, told the gang they was being raided and to assume the position. They all did, Boss, just like little lambs. They lined up against that wall thinking they was just going to the slammer for a few days, when they was really about to leave the world. Clipped 'em all right there with their backs turned. It was a massacre. We got Frank and Pete Gusenberg, Jim Clark, Jim May, Rhienie Schwimmer, and that eyes guy, you know the optician, Adam something, who's always hanging out with those guys. Bugs should'a been there. I don't know what happened to him."

"Criminey, McGurn," Capone fumed. "You're sure? Somebody's not just screwin' with you?"

"Naw, Boss. I'm sure. He wasn't there. I don't know, maybe he got wind of the operation, maybe he was just late gettin' there. Whatever it was, we missed him. But, look, there's going to be a big to-do made about this. They're already callin' it the St. Valentine's Day Massacre. We gotta lay low. Make sure they can't tie us to it."

"Yeah, yeah. I got it. You good?"

"Yeah. I got my blond alibi, you know. Married her so she couldn't testify. I'll give a shout in a day or two."

That night, Capone jerked suddenly awake. The room was dark. He'd pulled all the curtains before hitting the sack, and now it was impossible to see.

Something had awakened him—maybe that horror of a dream he was having. His heart was still hammering in his chest. What had it been? Oh, yeah. He was back in Chicago at that cold warehouse and he was looking at the massacre scene. As he stood there watching, the bloody corpses had suddenly risen and were all coming toward him with murder in their dead eyes. It was terrible.

Wiping a hand over his face, he turned on his side, hoping for sleep, but dreading it as well. What if he had another of those dreams? Suddenly, his breath quickened and his heart began pumping adrenaline throughout his body. Someone had just sat down on the foot of the bed. But no one was here. He knew that. Mae had gone to visit a friend in Tampa and had taken that yappy little mutt with her. None of the guys would've dared come in without knocking.

He froze in place, his heart hammering a tattoo against his chest. Maybe he was still dreaming. Yeah, that had to be it. He wasn't awake yet. Suddenly, a disembodied voice came from the foot of his bed.

"Naw, Scarface. You ain't asleep. I'm here. Just wanted to stop in and say hello."

Capone almost screamed as he jerked up to a

sitting position. Jeez! Could his heart beat any harder? Turning on the bedside lamp, he was posed to jump, but when light flooded the room he froze, and he wasn't sure, but he thought a faint scream might have escaped him.

There at the foot of his bed, legs crossed nonchalantly, blood covering gaping holes in his face, sat Jim Clark, Moran's right-hand man. Capone did let out a scream then, only it was more like a squeak, really.

"Clark! How...how? But you're supposed to be..."

"Dead? Oh, don't worry, Big Fellow. Youse got me, all right. I'm dead. At least my body is. Cold as a wedge. I'm on ice in the city morgue." He looked down at himself. "But, funny..." He examined his hand, turning it as if it were an unfamiliar thing. "Something of me is still here. And I had a great yen to come see you. I just thought about it and, hey, next thing I know, here I am. Not a bad way to travel, huh? Beats ankling it over. What's the matter, Big Guy? You look like you've seen a ghost. Oh, wait. ... You have!" The apparition broke into a rattling laugh. "Hee-hee. I slay me! No. Wait ... you did that!" He laughed harder, doubling over and slapping the side of the bed.

Drops of blood fell from his face and stained the white satin bedcovers.

The laughter stopped, just like a faucet being cut off. "You did do it, didn't you, Big Al? You set us up. You can't deny it, because I see it all. I don't know how, but that doesn't matter. I can see your goons, all gussied up like the heat, and all us bunnies lined up, not suspecting a thing. Yeah, you did it, all right.

"But you missed the main man, didn't you? Wonder what's that gonna do to your Mr. Big-plans for Chi-Town?"

Capone stared open-mouthed at the apparition sitting so calmly on his bed, as if it were an everyday thing for a bloody corpse to just walk in and take a seat.

"Wh-what do you want?" he stammered.

"Nothing, really. Just wanted to see the big man that put it all together. I stopped by to see Bugs before wingin' on down here, but he couldn't see me. You can, though, and even if the coppers never pinch you, it ain't gonna matter, Capone. 'Coz I'm gonna be here. You'll never know when I'll make a show. My old snozz—what's left of it—is gonna be mindin' your onions from now on. We're gonna get to be real pals, you and me. Hey, did you know when you turn pale like that it makes your scars stand out real purty?"

Chicago's Public Enemy No. 1 couldn't take it any longer. Maybe it was all the blood dripping onto his wife's once immaculate bedcovers. Maybe it was the teeth that showed through where the skin had been blown away by bullets. Whatever it was, he snapped. Suddenly the most feared man in all of Chi-Town, a man who'd personally sent men to their graves, started screaming, screaming like a little nancy boy crying for his mama.

Outside the suite, two of Capone's goons charged out of their rooms. With sleep in their eyes and guns in hands, hairy legs sprouting like trees from boxers, they looked at each other. Loud, high-pitched squeals were coming from the Boss's room. Sounded like a hog was getting slaughtered. The Big Fellow must've caught someone sneaking in the estate and was teaching her—judging from the pitch of the screams, it had to be a woman—a lesson.

Bursting into the room, they froze, guns held high, mouths agape. Huddled at the head of the bed, covers drawn to his chin, was the Boss. His eyes were focused on a point at the foot of the bed, and the high-pitched scream was coming from his mouth.

They looked around the room. Nothing.

"Boss! What is it? Boss!"

Capone's eyes left his focus spot just quick enough to give the goons a wild-eyed look. Both could see the terror in his baby blues.

"Do you see him? Get him out! Get him out!"

Clark's spirit splayed his lips in his gruesome smile. "They can't see me, fool. Only you can. Only you."

"Get him out! You've got to get him out. See him? He's there at the foot of the bed! He's bleeding on Mae's bedcovers!" Wildly, Capone pointed to the apparition sitting there, laughing at him.

The two goons shared a confused glance. The man they most feared and respected was screaming like a baby. The heels of his hands were pressed to each side of his head, and the look of horror on his face was frightening. "But, Boss. There's no one here. It's just us."

The laughing got louder. And louder. And just when Capone thought his heart would explode in fear, the apparition began to fade. "Don't worry, Al, baby. We're gonna be a pair from now on. I'm going to be your closest pal. You feel a ruffle through your hair, it ain't the wind. It'll be me, sayin' hello. A light touch on your shoulder. That's me. And every now and again,

I'll come for a real visit, just like tonight." With that, he was gone.

Capone stopped his screeching and looked at the now empty spot on the bed. He hugged himself, willing his body to stop trembling, and began to get control. He looked around the room. No Clark. He stared back at the white bed that had been covered in blood. It was pristine. He shook himself.

"Get out!" he croaked to his two minions. "Get out. I'm fine."

Outside in the hallway, the two gave each other a confused look.

"Whaddya think that was all about?" asked one.

The other shrugged. "Suppose the Boss has been hittin' the pipe?"

"Could be. Thought he was too savvy for that, but who knows? Sure was weird, though." They both shrugged and sauntered to their rooms.

Just as the ghost of Jim Clark accused, Al Capone was the orchestrator of the St. Valentine's Day Massacre, with Bugs Moran as the main target. Four of Capone's men entered a garage at 2122 N. Clark Street in Chicago, Moran's main liquor headquarters. Two of them were dressed as police officers, so their victims naturally thought it was a police raid. They dropped their guns and put their hands against the wall. When it was over, Capone's men had fired more than 150 bullets into their submissive targets.

The ensuing storm over the killings marshaled the resolve of the powers that be to bring down Al Capone. As for himself, Capone quite enjoyed the celebrity that followed the killings and was blissfully unaware that the St. Valentine's Day Massacre would eventually be his downfall.

Unable to bring him up on murder charges because of his airtight Florida alibi, the Feds looked for some other way to put him away. He was a visible enough—he lived like a celebrity and, on the advice of his publicist, he made no effort to hide. For example, when Charles Lindbergh made his famous trans-Atlantic flight in 1927, Capone was in the crowd that welcomed him in Chicago, even pushing through the crowd to shake the aviator's hand. He was extravagant in his kindness to strangers, particularly to struggling Italian-Americans, and was often cheered in the street.

But it was his Palm Island mansion that finally snagged him. He'd paid cash for it and Mae had gone on an extravagant decorating spree—all paid for in cash, none of which, of course, had been reported on his tax returns. In 1931, he was finally tried and convicted of tax evasion. He was sentenced to eleven years in prison—an eleven years in which he didn't fare so well.

In his youth, Capone had contracted syphilis, which reportedly began attacking his brain after he went to prison. He began experiencing dementia because of it. At least, that's what most historians claim.

They also attribute his obsession with the ghost of Jim Clark to this dementia. Others point out, however, that the dementia did not appear until after he was transferred to Alcatraz, the country's most brutal prison, in 1934. But it was just after the 1929 massacre that Clark's ghost began to hound him.

Reports are that many times in his Miami mansion, Capone's employees heard him pleading with the spirit to leave him be; to just go and leave him in peace. On several occasions, his bodyguards heard him screaming. When they burst into the room, they would be told by Capone that Clark's ghost was there. They, of course, saw nothing. In 1931, he even reportedly consulted a psychic to help rid him of his ghostly shadow.

The exorcism didn't seem to have taken. Many times in prison, he could be heard exhorting Jim Clark to leave him alone. At times he would refuse to leave his cell at all, and sometimes would be found crouching in a corner, babbling to himself like a baby, an ignominious position for the former head of the FBI's Most Wanted list.

After his release in 1940, Capone returned to his Miami estate to live out his days, alternating times of lucidity with those of complete dementia. And he was still obsessed with the ghost of Jim Clark. Many wonder about his obsession with only one ghost, pointing out that Capone had been responsible for the deaths of more than five hundred people. Why, then, was Jim Clark's the only spirit to haunt him? If the dementia were really responsible, would he not be haunted by the spirits of all those others? Is it not possible, ask some, that it's the other way around? That the constant harassment by this one entity was the cause of his dementia?

At one point in his life, Al Capone was the toughest tough guy around, but by the time of his death, he was a broken, beaten man. Suffering from a bout of bronchial pneumonia, he experienced a sudden brain hemorrhage on January 24, 1947. He died in Florida at age forty-eight, no longer a wanted man, but still very much a haunted man.

Ghostly Stars of the Tampa Theater

Ghostly Stars of the Tampa Theater

The Tampa Theater was opened in 1926 as one of the country's most elaborate movie palaces. A sparkling jewel set into the Tampa landscape, it was designed by famed theater architect John Eberson, who innovated the "atmospheric" style of theater design. Eberson often wintered in Tampa, and he credited Florida with inspiring this particular design style. The colorful scenes he found in Tampa, Miami, and Palm Beach, he said, evoked visions of Italian gardens, Spanish patios, Persian shrines, and French formal gardens.

Many of these dreamy elements found their way into Eberson's design of the Tampa Theater. Theatergoers stepped from the heat of the Tampa streets and were instantly transported to the coolness of a romantic Mediterranean courtyard. In the terrazzo-tiled terrace, they found Romanesque statues of gods and goddesses, ornate columns, mischievous gargoyles peeping down from the balcony, and a profusion of flowers. Overhead, a nighttime sky twinkled with stars. And it was all wrapped in a delicious chill—the Tampa was one of the first buildings in the city to have air-conditioning.

It's little wonder that the Tampa Theater, like movie palaces around the country, was enormously popular. For the first time in history, common folk could enjoy an opulence that heretofore they could only imagine.

For the price of one thin dime, they could escape the harsh reality of their lives and inhabit a fantasy land where they were treated like royalty by platoons of uniformed ushers and attendants. Oh! The sights they took in! From the wonder of moving pictures to the magic of the mighty thousand-pipe Wurlitzer rising from the depths of the stage, it was an experience they couldn't get enough of. By the end of the 1920s, more then 90 million Americans were going to the movies every week.

For decades, the theater remained a Tampa treasure. Scores of citizens grew up within her walls, sitting wide-eyed as cowboys and Indians battled it out before them, then splatting the lady two rows ahead with spitballs; stealing their first kisses in the dark recesses of the balcony; and then later on, maybe even popping the question there.

Ah, but time marches on, and by the 1960s, America had evolved into a suburban nation, devastating downtown business districts across the country. Too, the popularity of that newfangled television caused a dramatic drop in movie attendance. Hey, why pay when you could stay home and watch *I Love Lucy* for free? The Tampa Theater closed down in the early 1970s, like most other fine movie palaces in the country.

But many of the others were demolished before their historic value was recognized. Fortunately, the good people of Tampa were more astute. Committees were formed. Plans were made. City leaders politicked. And soon a deal was reached. The city agreed to rescue the Tampa.

Much needed repairs and restorations were completed, and the theater reopened in 1978. Since that time, it has become a success story, presenting more than six hundred events a year, including new and classic movies, live concerts, and all types of special events.

With such a storied history, you'd expect the Tampa Theater to have at least one otherworldly entity roaming its darkened hallways. Well, despair not, for the Tampa does, indeed, have more than one ghostly spirit.

The most famous ghost of the Tampa Theater is that of Foster "Fink" Finley, the theater's obsessive-compulsive projectionist. Fink began working at the Tampa in 1930 and quickly became devoted to the theater, reportedly spending more time there than he did with his wife and family. He did, in fact, live and die there. You see, Fink experienced a fatal heart attack in 1965 in the theater's projection room.

As so often happens when someone dies in such a manner, Fink's spirit has remained on the premises. Not long after he died, the new projectionist reported one day that as he entered the projection room and tried to pull the door closed behind him, someone—or something—pulled back on it to prevent it from closing. When he investigated, there was no one there.

He reported other mysterious incidents in the ensuing years. Remember, this was back in the reel-to-reel days, and there were times when the projectionist had to pay close attention to cues in the film in order to switch projectors. Often, when he was showing a film and those times neared, he said he would hear the door to the generator open—though the door never actually opened—and, momentarily, the loud noise of the generator. It was as if old Fink had been out doing a bit of work and was returning in time to keep the movie running smoothly.

Employees report that Fink is a mischievous ghost, often sneaking away tools or other items. If asked, however, he will return them, though days later and somewhere else in the theater. He's credited with the sound of keys rattling, tapping employees on their shoulders, and the mysterious opening and closing of doors.

It's a definite possibility that Fink's not the only one perpetrating these pranks. At least two other spirits are reported to be spending their eternity in the Tampa. The most interesting, perhaps, is the spirit of the Lady in Waiting.

This apparition, glimpsed by patrons and contacted by local ghost hunters, is the spirit of a young woman who lived in Tampa from the late 1800s until her death in the 1920s. When the Florida paranormal group S.P.I.R.I.T.S. of St. Petersburg demonstrated its abilities to a local television station, the Lady in Waiting appeared to several of the group's "sensitives" and communicated with them.

Dressed in white, she indicated that she knew she was deceased, that she lived in the late 1800s, and could remember up to the 1920s. The ghost trackers got the impression that she was a lady of expensive tastes. She referred to herself as "Jezebel," and "Jessie," though this seemed to be a character comment rather than her name.

Perhaps she was being sarcastic in that self comment, for she indicated that she had been a quite attractive woman, pursued by many men who gave her expensive gifts. The town's women were jealous and sometimes cast slurs upon her good name. Despite that, the woman reported being very much in love with the handsome man to whom she was engaged. It's he for whom she waits, often standing in the balcony looking down on the crowds in the auditorium or pacing back and forth amid the lobby crowds.

It's not exactly known why she haunts the theater, though she reports being killed one night by a runaway horse and buggy while crossing Franklin Street—the street in front of the Tampa. Perhaps it was just natural for her spirit to come here, where she would have ghostly company. The psychics report that she is often accompanied by a silent, thin gentleman dressed in some type of uniform.

Paranormal groups consider the Tampa Theater to be one of the country's most active supernatural venues. They hold open the possibility that many spirits live there besides the ones currently known. In addition, photos and videos taken here are filled with "orbs," unexplained balls of lights that most paranormal researchers consider to be ghostly manifestations, and electronic equipment used by researchers constantly register the presence of otherworldly spirits.

It really should be no surprise that there are numerous entities residing within the ornate walls of the Tampa Theater. Its history is the history of Tampa. Ask anyone who grew up here about the Tampa and there's a good chance they can tell you how it's touched their lives. It's been a happy place for many people, so why not think that some spirits might find their way back there. And besides, if you were a ghost, where would you rather hang out? In some dark and dank mansion or cemetery? Nah. Bet you'd be like old Fink and the Lady in Waiting. You'd prefer a place full of lights, action, and life.

The Star-crossed Lovers of Don CeSar

The Star-crossed Lovers of Don CeSar

Young Thomas Rowe took his seat in the theater just as the curtain was rising. He had come to the opera tonight expecting only to enjoy the show one of his fellow students was raving about, and nothing more. The moment the stage lights came up, however, he knew his life was forever changed.

There, in the spotlight, stood the woman of his dreams. A tumble of iridescent ebony hair framed her face and breasts, then fell away down her curving back. Her tawny complexion spoke of a foreign descent, Spanish perhaps. She had luscious red lips and soulful dark eyes that he swore were looking right at him. And her voice! When she opened that luscious mouth and sang, his heart threatened to jump right out of his chest. Grabbing up his program, he thumbed it until he found her name—not far in, since she was playing the starring role. Lucinda! Her name was Lucinda. Lovely, luscious Lucinda.

Mesmerized by her beauty, Thomas only peripherally absorbed the opera's plot of star-crossed lovers Maritana, played by lovely Lucinda, and Don CeSar, played by…someone, who find happiness in the end. Although he was just a poor American student studying here in London and she was obviously a rising star, he was determined they would meet. That determination is what propelled the brash young man, hat in hand, to the back door of the theater.

"My lovely Maritana," he said, bowing elaborately, as she stepped into the alleyway. "Don CeSar at your service. May I escort you to your destination, or, perhaps you'd like to stop for a light supper somewhere?"

Startled, Lucinda stepped back. She gave him a coy smile and appraised him with those big, dark eyes that made his heart flutter. "Why, sir, you are quite bold."

"That I am, mistress, and for that I apologize. But from the moment I first laid eyes on you, I knew I must meet you. Please forgive a man made speechless by your beauty and your talent."

She smiled again, a reply on her lips. But before she could speak, they were descended upon by a rather loud woman. A small, dapper man tagged along behind.

"Lucinda! What are you doing loitering back here? You could be assaulted. Or accosted by strange men," the woman said, giving Thomas a nose-turned-up look. "Come, dear. We must get home."

"Yes, Mother. I'm coming." Lucinda quickly turned back to Thomas, and with a secret smile, whispered. "Your boldness, Don CeSar, is somewhat appealing. Meet me tomorrow around 2:00 at the fountain in Trafalgar Square. I shall only have a few minutes, but perhaps then you can tell me your real name." She smiled over her shoulder once more as she disappeared around the corner of the building.

The next afternoon, Thomas, dressed in his best suit, arrived at Trafalgar Square an hour before the appointed time, too anxious to hang around his small apartment any longer. As he strolled around the square, he ruminated on his good fortune. Why, just a couple of years from now, they'd be entering the 1900s. A new century and his future—and the promise of young love—all ahead of him. True, he didn't have much to offer his lovely Lucinda right now, but that wouldn't last long. He knew as soon as his studies were complete and he returned to his beloved Florida, his fortune would be made. Surely

Lucinda's snobby mother would see his promise and respond to his complete and utter devotion to her daughter.

He turned back toward the fountain, and stopped as his heart skipped a beat. There she was, her black hair a halo around her bemused face.

"Don CeSar," she held out her hand. He took it in his and bowed elegantly.

"Maritana."

They sat on the edge of the fountain and talked. He told her of his dreams, the plans he had for when he returned to America, and about how he knew there was a fortune to be made in Florida real estate. She spoke of her singing, which she loved, and her belief in true love—how she believed that even in death, true lovers would meet somewhere on a higher plane. She also talked of the strictness of her parents, which she loathed. Her mother was the worst, always keeping tabs on her. Yes, Lucinda knew she had a wonderful career ahead of her, but sometimes she wasn't sure if it was worth giving up the rest of her life.

The couple met at the fountain at the same time every day. And every day they greeted each other with their affectionate nicknames for each other. Each time

time as he left, Thomas knew he was even deeper in love. He was certain Lucinda felt the same. So, finally, after weeks of clandestine rendezvous, he insisted on calling upon her at home to plead his case to her mother. Big mistake.

Lucinda's mother was a formidable woman, driven by her snobbery and by her devotion to her daughter's career. Nothing, absolutely nothing, was going to get in the way of that, certainly not this lowly American student with no money and no prospects. She banished him from her home and forbade Lucinda to see him.

For weeks, he tried to change the infuriating woman's mind, but she was resolute. Finally, one day, a tearful Lucinda met him at their fountain, where they still rendezvoused daily, exchanging passionate love words and making promises of what their life together would be like. It was impossible, she cried. Her mother would not relent. Defying her would mean turning her back on her family, something she could not do. This, she said, would be their last meeting. He tried to change her mind, but she was as stubborn as her mother. They kissed sweetly, desperately, and parted that day, never again to see each other. At least not in this life.

Thomas completed his studies in London and returned to America. He set about making his fortune in Florida real estate, just as he had told Lucinda he would. Soon he was a millionaire—someone with money and prospects, someone worthy of his lovely Maritana. For two years, he wrote passionate pleas to Lucinda, telling her of his new situation and begging her to see him. But for two long years, his letters were returned to him unopened.

Then one day in the post, there it was. On creamy white stationery. A letter from the lovely Lucinda, his Maritana. Eagerly he opened it, and elation quickly dissolved to despair.

My beloved CeSar:

Time is infinite. I wait for you by our fountain, to share our timeless love forever.

Our destiny is time.

Your Maritana

Reading the words, he knew in his soul that she was gone, knew that her letter was telling him that they would someday meet on another plane, in a time and a place where their love could finally be free.

Thomas Rowe went on with his life, building his fortune and even taking a wife. But he never forgot the Spanish beauty who had stolen his heart and taken it with her to that higher plane.

Finally, in 1925, Thomas began building his dream hotel, a resort that would stand as a remembrance to his lost love, his Maritana. He first hired famed architect Henry DuPont, but fired him because his design was too plain. Thomas wanted a monument. Something striking. Something people would point to and marvel over.

He hired a new architect and worked closely with him to make his dream come true. Out of the sands of St. Petersburg grew a grand flamingo-pink castle. Mediterranean-style and accented with Moorish bell towers and majestic turrets, the hotel originally was estimated to cost $1.2 million. It ran almost 300 percent over budget.

That mattered not to Rowe, for money should be no object when love is involved. He named his pink castle the Don CeSar. In the center of the courtyard, he built a replica of the London fountain, the rendezvous fountain, where he'd spent so many happy times with the true love of his life. He opened the hotel with an extravagant gala on January 16, 1928. More than fifteen hundred guests enjoyed dining in the fifth-floor restaurant and dancing in the grand ballroom.

"The Don" quickly became the hot spot for the Roaring Twenties in-crowd, with celebrity guests such as Al Capone, Tallulah Bankhead, and Clarence Darrow making it a favorite party place. F. Scott Fitzgerald was so taken with the resort that he wrote about it in many of his books, once referring to it as a "hotel in an island wilderness." It was, it seems, a favorite dry-out place for the often soused Zelda.

Rowe loved the hotel that love had built, and for the next twelve years he rarely left it. With a suite on the fifth floor, he could often be seen sporting a Panama hat as he made his rounds, greeting guests and engaging them in conversation, always ending with an order to just let the staff know if they needed anything at all.

The Don CeSar reigned as a vacation hot spot until 1940, when Rowe suddenly collapsed in the hotel's ornate lobby. Refusing hospitalization, he was carried to his room, where medical care was brought to him. Realizing that his time was close, the childless Rowe insisted that his will be amended to leave the Don CeSar to his staff, the people he believed could best carry on his dream.

Unfortunately, the nurses there refused to sign as witnesses, believing Rowe incapable of making such a monumental decision. The Don went to Rowe's estranged wife, who let it fall to disrepair. After the attack on Pearl Harbor on December 7, 1941, its operations suffered the effects of cancellations, rotating supplies, and loss of employees as people were drafted into the military. In 1942, it was sold to the U.S. Army for just $450,000. It was turned into a convalescent center for battle-fatigued World War II airmen. After the war, the government stripped it and used it as a regional office, but when, in 1967, needed repairs proved too costly, it was abandoned.

The once immaculate hotel languished on the sands of St. Petersburg beach. Efforts to raze it were met with stiff opposition by residents. It soon became a graffiti-covered eyesore, until the early 1970s, when St. Petersburg revitalization discovered the Don CeSar. And it was then that things got strange.

When renovations began, workers began reporting a distinguished silver-haired man, wearing a tailored suit with one of those starched old-timey collars, hanging around the work site. He never interfered, they said. He simply watched their progress as they sweated in the Florida sun. They asked management about the guy, wondering if he had authorization to be there, but no one seemed to know who he was.

It's not certain who finally put two and two together and figured out that the spirit of Thomas Rowe had returned, perhaps to take delight in the fact that his hotel was being restored to its former glory. Once renovations were complete, he began appearing in the lobby, Panama hat perched on his silver hair, suit and tie in immaculate condition, tending, it seems, to his old duties as host. There are even reports that he has interacted with his guests, inquiring about the weather, the enjoyment of their stay, and their satisfaction with the amenities, always urging them to consult the staff if they needed anything at all. By all accounts, he is courtly and kindly, and though his sudden disappearing act surely gives a start, no one ever reports being frightened.

The story doesn't end there. Since the 1980s, there have been numerous reports of a dark-haired beauty who frequents the Don CeSar. Wearing clothes of another era, she has a tumble of ebony hair and a strikingly lovely face that often wears an expression of bemusement. In the first years of her appearance, she was seen sitting at the hotel fountain, sometimes alone, sometimes with the kindly man sitting next to her. He would hold her hand and smile into her eyes, occasionally brushing her lips with a tender kiss. Guests drifting by sometimes mentioned hearing a whispering of "Maritana" or "Don CeSar."

Today, the Don CeSar once again reigns as a pretty pink playground for the rich and famous, with celebrities as diverse as Britney Spears and Bill Clinton coming here to party. Now called the Don CeSar Beach Resort and Spa, Rowe's hotel sports the AAA Four-Diamond Maritana Grille, a second swimming pool with surrounding tropical gardens, and a full-service spa—four thousand square feet of additional space.

Despite all these "improvements," there has been one tragic loss. During recent renovations, the rendezvous fountain was done away with, putting a crimp in the couples' trysting. Ah, but love will overcome.

Today, the couple is sometimes spotted down by the beach, holding hands, engrossed in each other. When guests spot them strolling together, they profess a need to avoid the lovers, not from fear, but rather from respect for a love that has found freedom on a higher plane.

But Ma!

But Ma!

According to news stories of the day, which came from FBI reports and theories, not only did Ma Barker raise four really diabolical sons, but she also headed the Karpis-Barker gang and masterminded their three-year crime spree. That's the FBI's story, and they're stickin' to it.

Arizona Donnie "Kate" Barker never really had much going for her. Born in the Ozark Mountains of Missouri, she became enamored with the outlaw life early on. As a young girl, her greatest thrill was watching Jesse James ride past. She was reportedly devastated when he was killed.

A tad on the dumpy side and not terribly attractive, she was definitely not your proverbial farmer's daughter. However, by age twenty-one, she'd found a husband in a farm laborer named George Barker. The two spent their early married years eking a living out of the stingy Missouri farmland. In this dirt poor existence, Ma began birthing her brood of hardened criminals.

First came Herman; next was Lloyd; then Arthur,

also known as "Doc"; and finally there was Mama's little angel, Freddie, the youngest and her favorite. The boys were still just little whippersnappers when, in 1910, they began turning up on police blotters. And Ma was always there, ready to do whatever it took—scream, cry, cajole—to get her little boys out of trouble.

The family moved to Tulsa, Oklahoma, in 1915, and began their life of crime in earnest. According to FBI theory, Ma was a woman who liked easy living. She yearned for the good things in life—nice clothes, expensive furniture, fast cars. Tired of the impoverished life George offered, she encouraged—nay, abetted—her sons in their chosen career as bad guys.

From the petty crimes they'd committed as kids, the boys graduated to big-time crime, starting out with bank robberies. And, said the FBI, Ma was right there with them. She plotted their capers and mapped out getaway routes for them. She then stayed home, crying and praying that they wouldn't get caught.

Ma and her boys weren't the only ones who had chosen crime as a career. The late 1920s and early 1930s were a golden age for bank robbers and other criminals, with the emergence of such famous perpetrators as Charles "Pretty Boy" Floyd, John Dillinger, Bonnie and Clyde, and George "Baby Face" Nelson.

The gangs raced around the country robbing banks, and in between jobs, they lived it up, renting expensive apartments, buying fast cars, and generally wreaking havoc. Ma's boys proved to be a ruthless lot. By the early 1920s, their penchant for killing without provocation had earned them the moniker of the "Bloody Barkers."

Although law enforcement groups at the time were overwhelmed by the sheer numbers of the bad guys, they did have some success. In 1920, Doc, the gang's leader, was captured after shooting a night watchman. He was sentenced to life imprisonment. Lloyd was sentenced to twenty-five years in 1922 for mail theft, and Fred, Ma's baby, was sent to prison for killing a policeman while stealing a car.

The authorities may have felt pretty smug about having incarcerated the Bloody Barkers, but they were no match for Ma. She badgered parole boards, wardens, and even the governor. She was so persistent, in fact, that she won a release for Fred, and was even able to get a governor's pardon for Doc.

The Barkers did experience one loss. In 1927, Herman committed suicide after being severely injured in a shootout with the police. The gang regrouped, however, and in 1931 teamed with Albert "Creepy" Karpis, whom Fred had met during his unfortunate incarceration.

The Karpis-Barker gang became one of the most formidable gangs of the 1930s. They robbed banks and hijacked mail deliveries, leaving a bloody trail of bodies behind them. In 1933, they graduated from banks to people. The gang kidnapped Minnesota millionaire William Hamm, a caper that netted them $100,000 in ransom money. It was so successful that the gang decided to go for it again. They abducted Minnesota banker Edward Bremer and brought in another $200,000.

The "great crime wave" of 1933 and 1934, perpetrated by the Barkers and other criminals, spurred the formation of a federal police force, which became the FBI. Along with local police forces, the FBI began to methodically hunt down these public enemies. In 1934 alone, they tracked down and killed John Dillinger, Bonnie and Clyde, Pretty Boy Floyd, and Baby Face Nelson.

With those guys out of the way, the FBI set its sights on the Karpis-Barker gang. As a fledgling law enforcement group, the FBI was almost as ruthless as the criminals it pursued. Agents tracked down the twenty-five members of the Barker gang. One by one, they were either captured or killed. Doc was captured on January 8, 1935, and sent to Alcatraz, where he was killed in an escape attempt four years later.

One week later, the FBI tracked down Ma and Fred, holed up in a cottage in Lake Weir, Florida. They sent one agent to the front door. He knocked. Ma came to the door. Seconds later, Fred stepped out with a machine gun and began shooting. The two retreated into the house, and Fred continued shooting.

The gun battle lasted five hours and is reportedly the longest gun battle of all time. When the shooting from inside the house stopped, agents entered and found both Ma and Fred dead. Ma was found in the upstairs bedroom, shot three times, her machine gun, still hot to the touch, clutched to her breast. There was more than $10,000 found in her pocketbook.

Despite public outrage at the criminal spree, the FBI worried about its public relations image, and how hunting down and killing a dumpy grandmother would make the agency look. So, the story was revised a bit. According to the official account, Ma Barker had been the mastermind of all the gang's activities, from robbing banks to kidnapping millionaires. She was, it turned out, a clever, greedy, and ruthless woman.

Ma Barker should sue.

Come to find out, Ma was nothing like her "Bloody Mama" image. Instead of being the criminal genius the FBI made her out to be, Ma was, in reality, mostly just a doting mother. According to Alvin Karpis, who was the last public enemy to be tracked down, the FBI portrayal of Ma Barker was the "most ridiculous story in the annals of crime." According to him, Ma wasn't the leader of the gang nor did she mastermind any of the gang's exploits. She was, of course, aware of the gang's criminality, but all she did was travel with the gang, acting as a mother to her sons and other members of the gang. After the shootout, Karpis threatened to kill FBI head J. Edgar Hoover the same way Fred and Ma had been killed.

As you might expect of a house with such a bloody past, the Lake Weir house of Ma and Freddie Barker, riddled with more than thirty-five hundred bullets, is rumored to be inhabited by spirits. Reportedly, on dark evenings, the sound of a card game being played—the shuffling of the deck and the sound of cards being slapped down—can be heard. There's also the sound of voices—one female—although no one has been able to understand what's being said. Hmmm…"Clean up that mess," maybe? You know, once a mother always a mother.

Bookin' It

Bookin' It

Does the spirit of writer Jack Kerouac haunt his favorite bookstore? Many people believe so.

Haslam's Book Store in St. Petersburg first opened its doors in 1933. It was the middle of the Great Depression, and to increase business, owners Mary and Charles Haslam sold handicrafts, roses, doilies, and used magazines in addition to books. The store survived and grew, and by the 1960s, it was a thriving business.

Jack Kerouac came to St. Petersburg under duress in 1966. He and his wife were living with his mother, and when she left their Lowell, Massachusetts, home to avoid the cold winters, they went with her. The voice of the Beat generation didn't give St. Petersburg a ringing endorsement, often calling it "Salt Petersburg, the town of the newly wed and the living dead."

Kerouac was only in his mid-forties by the time he reached St. Petersburg, but an addiction to Johnnie Walker Red and Benzedrine had taken its toll on his body, his mind, and his spirit. He'd used up his youth hard and fast in a revved-up, wild, and desperate road trip in search of enlightenment. He was the first to howl "Sex, Drugs, and Rock 'n' Roll," the battle cry of disenfranchised youth everywhere. Except, of course, his cry was made before rock 'n' roll came about, so he'd cried for bebop instead.

Bebop jazz had, in fact, been the inspiration for his stream-of-consciousness writing style, a style Kerouac called spontaneous prose. He would start with a thought, a sentence, or an idea, and play it for all its essence. Then he'd move on to the next, feeling a rhythm build and working off it like riffs on a guitar, ignoring the sanity of punctuation and drawing in his reader with the cadence of his beat.

He was a prolific writer, and a fast one, having written *On The Road* in just three, coffee-and Benzedrine-soaked weeks. In addition to his unorthodox punctuation, he wrote the entire manuscript in one long, continuous roll. Perhaps that's why it took seven years to sell it!

Published in 1957, this mostly autobiographical, but embellished, story of his travels with friends became the defining work of the Beat generation and made Kerouac the king of that generation, a title he despised. The fame it brought him may ultimately have been his downfall.

By the time he arrived in St. Petersburg, his publishing days were behind him. The road trip was in the rearview mirror, and enlightenment had eluded him. He was here, settled in a strange town, angry and disillusioned. He drank heavily, saturating an already diseased liver, and spent days locked away in his 10th Avenue home, eyes glued to the boob tube.

But it wasn't all bad. He'd found a couple of friends who dropped by to talk, and he'd found succor in the local bookstore, where he could browse the shelves and immerse himself in words.

Charles Haslam didn't recognize the disheveled man as a famous writer when he first entered the store. It wasn't until later, after the man had spent quite some time browsing through the shelves and left, that Charles noticed the books of Jack Kerouac had been pulled from the bottom shelf and placed right at eye level. As he was replacing them, he happened to glance at the photograph on the back panel of *On The Road*.

Aha. Now he understood. Sad, he thought, that a man such as him should be in such a condition. He had heard, of course, that Kerouac had moved here, and, too, had heard of the unflattering comments he'd made about St. Petersburg. If he didn't want to be here, thought Haslam, then he should just leave. Didn't need him around messing up the shelves if that's the way he felt.

Kerouac wasn't going anywhere, and he seemed to enjoy the bookstore, for he visited often, spending hours browsing through the ever-growing inventory of books. An ongoing argument arose between him and Haslam about the store's alphabetical arrangement of books. Seems Kerouac's books always ended up on the bottom shelves, a problem he would remedy each time he came, moving them to a shelf at eye level and facing them forward. And each time, Haslam would move them back.

The put-out store owner spoke to the writer about the problem several times, asking him to leave the books where they were, and many times a lively discussion about book placement ensued. Neither would yield his position.

Of course, the point was rendered moot (or was it?), on October 21, 1969, when Kerouac suffered a fatal abdominal hemorrhage.

Many people suspect, the owners of Haslam's included, that Kerouac is still overseeing the placement of his books here. Since his death, Haslam's has greatly expanded. With more than three hundred thousand books, it is now the state's largest independent bookstore. So if Kerouac is here, at least he's got plenty to do.

It was after the store's expansion into the building next door in the 1970s that weird things started happening, things that led employees and owners to believe that a spirit had moved in. Customers and employees began reporting incidences where they felt the presence of someone when there was no one there. At times, someone would feel the tap of an invisible hand on his shoulder. There were sudden cold spots, and most tellingly, books would mysteriously fly off the shelves. On several occasions, it was Kerouac's books that fell.

It happened to Ray Hinst, third-generation owner of Haslam's. A few years back, Hinst says, he was restocking the fiction shelves, when he heard the distinctive sound of a book hitting the floor behind him. When he turned around to look, a copy of Kerouac's *On The Road* lay at his feet. It was just past midnight and he was there alone. Or so he thought.

The haunting of Haslam's has piqued the interest of local paranormal research groups, who've visited with their equipment and "sensitives," people who are able to feel and see otherworldly entities. They say, indeed, the place has ghosts, and yes, they believe Jack Kerouac is one of them.

The research team has determined that the benevolent spirit of a middle-aged man with salt and pepper hair looks remarkably like the photograph of Kerouac on the back cover of *On the Road*. The spirit is elusive, however, choosing not to speak. He follows the group around and watches the activity with a bemused expression on his face. The team says he likes the books and really enjoys being there. It's a place where he found comfort in life and seems to still find it in death.

In addition to Kerouac, the team says they've encountered a little boy spirit, who likes to take the books off the shelves, and a little girl, who wanders around the store confused. They believe she's the spirit of a little girl who was killed in a car wreck in front of the store. They also report seeing a man and woman who sit close together reading.

Hinst says he doesn't object to the presence of

these spirits, as long as they're not scaring off the customers. He can "live and let live," he says, although "live" might not be exactly the right word. He does note that perhaps there's a good reason Kerouac seems to be leaving the books on their shelves. What with all that expansion and the addition of thousands books, his works now have better placement—right about eye level.

Ashley's Restaurant

Ashley's Restaurant

When Ethel Allen stepped into Jack's Tavern that morning, several folks took notice. The teenager was certainly a looker, with that head of long blonde hair and a face dominated by big blue eyes. Those eyes, fringed by long, dark lashes, held the look of a girl on the cusp of womanhood. As she bounced across the floor to the bar, many there wondered at her father's insistence that she work here. She was, after all, only fifteen years old—old enough to cause trouble, too young to handle it.

Jack's Tavern had opened just the year before—New Year's Eve 1933—in celebration of the end of Prohibition. Since that time, it had been a continuous party. There was drinking, socializing, and dancing. Jack's even had one of them newfangled jukeboxes, the first ever in Brevard County!

Owner Jack Allen did his best to keep things in line, but after years of drinking in dark back rooms, the exuberance at no longer having to hide often got out of hand. There were frequent brawls and many domestic incidents—where a spouse would get angry or jealous and cause trouble. So far, no one had been seriously hurt, but it was just a matter of time.

Allen knew people often questioned his sanity at putting young Ethel to work here. He understood their concern, but in his mind, he was keeping her close, where he could keep his eye on her. She had been a beautiful child, and she was growing into an even more beautiful woman. He'd raised her as best he could after her mother had left, keeping close tabs on her comings and goings, and not allowing her to get silly ideas of going out with boys or wearing face paint. He wasn't a hard man, but he'd lost his wife to another man and he had no intention of losing his only daughter as well.

"Hey, Daddy," Ethel said as she tied an apron around her small waist. She went on tiptoe to give him a quick kiss on the cheek.

"Hi, sweetie. I have you assigned to tables 3, 4, and 5. You'll be taking over from Lana. It's been really busy, so hurry up and get ready." He saw her eyes scan the crowd as if looking for someone, and felt a niggle of worry in the pit of his stomach.

Distracted, Ethel nodded, picked up her tray, and

glided out to the main floor. Her eyes still scanned the faces of the tavern's considerable crowd because she was, in fact, searching for someone. She was hopefully looking for the gentleman who had been in two nights ago. He'd said he planned to come by tonight. And he'd said he would request her station.

She smiled to herself. The guy was a dreamboat. He was older—at least twenty-five. And he had curly, black hair, with dreamy blue eyes and dimples when he smiled. He'd flashed a money clip filled with cash and talked about living in Hollywood, where there were movie stars everywhere. He'd said she was beautiful enough to be a star, too.

Jeepers! That was her dream—to see herself on the big silver screen. She had seen every movie ever made! Posters of all her favorite stars covered the walls of her room. She especially liked that new type of movie they called the "slasher movie." They were so deliciously scary!

And that's the type of movie this guy said he made. And he'd said he was looking for girls to star in them. She'd been so excited that she thought she'd never make it through the next two days. But here it was Friday, finally. She hoped he showed up soon, or else she might pee on herself out of excitement.

She jumped in and began working her tables, deftly avoiding the pinches and touches inflicted by some of the men who'd had a few too many. She weaved in and out, back and forth, tray held high, working up a sheen of sweat.

She was so busy, she almost forgot why she had such an edge of excitement in her belly, but then, suddenly, there he was. He was sitting at table 3 and smiling up at her. Her heart skipped. Finally! She flashed him her biggest smile and approached the table.

"Hello. How are you?"

"I'm very well, Ethel. It looks like you're really busy."

"Yes, we are, Mr…"

"Ah, now, remember I told you to call me Jim."

She beamed even brighter at him. "Jim," she said tentatively.

"That's better. Well, now, I was wondering if you'd had time to think about what we discussed before?"

She bobbed her blonde head. "Oh, yes…uh, Jim! It's just all I could think about for the whole two days!"

"Good, good. And what do you think? Are you going to do it? Are you going to let me make you the star of my next slasher movie?"

Ethel took a furtive look around to ensure that no one had heard what he'd said. Everyone was bustling about. No one was paying any attention to her and the good looking man. Good thing Johnny wasn't here. He'd be all over her, demanding to know just who the guy was and what he wanted. And her father! Thank goodness for all the business. He was too busy drawing up beers and slinging drinks to notice what she was up to.

"Yes! Yes, I am! I can't leave just yet, though. I have to finish out the shift. But I'm all packed. I'll change clothes in the restroom, and then I can slip away while Daddy is closing up. I'll call him once we get to Hollywood to let him know I'm OK."

The guy nodded. "That sounds good. And have you told anyone else? Anyone at all?"

Shaking her head vehemently, she said, "No one. I promise! I haven't told anyone."

"That's good." He smiled benignly at her. "Now, bring me a Jack and Coke, and we'll plan to meet at the spot we discussed at, say, around midnight?"

"Yes, sir. Midnight sounds good. I'll be there, I promise!"

As he watched her bounce away, he began planning out the opening scenes of his next slasher movie, the one starring Miss Ethel Allen, the young Florida ingénue. Bloodcurdling screams! Unspeakable horrors! Oh, yes, it was going to be a killer, all right, he chuckled. A real killer.

Ethel Allen walked out of Jack's Tavern that night and was never seen alive again. Her poor, mutilated body was found days later on the banks of the Indian River, miles away, near the town of Eau Gallie. It was, said the old *Cocoa Tribune*, "the most mystifying and brutal murder case ever to occur within the confines of Brevard County." And, indeed, it was mystifying, for the murder of Ethel Allen was never solved.

Fast forward to modern times. Jack's Tavern is now Ashley's Restaurant, an establishment better known for its ghosts than for its food. It is, in fact, one of the most haunted places in Florida.

Many people believe the spirit haunting Ashley's is that of Ethel Allen, who was murdered in 1934. Though her body was found, the homicide remains unsolved. Many people believe she may still be at Ashley's. Customers and employees alike have reported a wide range of happenings here, from the mild to the down right aggressive.

The women's bathroom is a particularly haunted area. There have been numerous reports of an ethereal young woman who emerges from one of the stalls, then just disappears. She flicks lights on and off in the bar, often breaks things in the kitchen, and projects an overpowering presence to employees.

Oh, and that's not all. Some women report feeling as if they're being choked when walking down the hallway to the restroom. There also have been reports of shoulder tapping and, every now and again, a push from an unseen hand. One particularly terrified lady reported that when she looked into the restroom mirror to refresh her lipstick, instead of her own familiar face, she saw a stranger's face—that of a younger woman! As she stared, the face slowly disappeared. Well aware that she was in a haunted establishment, she dropped her lipstick and ran.

So, what do you think? Has Ethel Allen come back to haunt Ashley's Restaurant, the place where in life she felt safe? And was that her face in the mirror? Checking her makeup, perhaps? Making sure she's ready for her closeup?

Cassadaga

Cassadaga

When George Colby was a young boy growing up in New York, it was prophesied to him that he would become the founder of a spiritual community in the South. Colby grew up to become a talented medium, and sure enough, in 1875, his spirit guide, a Native American named Seneca, led him to Florida. Trekking through the wilderness of Central Florida, Colby was guided to an area with an unusually high energy level. This, the spirits told him, would be the site of a winter spiritualist camp, where psychics, mediums, astrologists, and other spiritualists could come to escape the frigid northern winters and live in peace without interference from the outside world.

He homesteaded thirty-five acres, and right off the bat, the area proved to be high in healing energy. Colby reportedly was suffering with tuberculosis when he arrived here, but after drinking an elixir from the spring running through his new land, he soon found he was cured.

When the camp was first started, back in 1894,

visitors would come and set up tents for their stay at Colby's Cassadaga—a Native American word meaning "rocks beneath the waters." As the camp grew, a church, meeting hall, and some houses were built. Many visitors decided to stay year-round.

Word spread—or perhaps the news was sent around by telepathy—of how spiritualists were coming together and living in peace in this little place in the middle of Florida. Psychics and mediums flocked to Cassadaga. They put out discreet little signs, offering their assistance in dealing with all types of matters, from star-crossed love to the opportunity to speak with Aunt Bessie, who'd passed last year.

They also offered teachings in Spiritualism, a religion or philosophy based upon the belief that life continues after the "change called death," and that those who have passed over can communicate with the living through mediums. All this one hundred years before anyone ever coined the phrase "New Age!"

Today, Cassadaga is known as the Psychic Center of the World, and is the oldest active religious community in the Southeast. It occupies fifty-five acres and is designated a Historical District on the National Register of Historic Places. Its narrow streets and tin-roofed cottages dating back to the 1920s take you back to a simpler time. That is, if your "simpler time" included talking with the dead.

Reputed to be located within an energy vortex, Cassadaga is one of the most spiritually-active places on Earth. People come from all over the world to study here, to have "readings" by psychics and mediums, and to receive guidance from the great beyond.

Got a problem that only someone in touch with the next world can solve? Want to contact your dead mother to find out if she's finally at peace? Need to know where crazy Uncle Jess hid the will? Then you should come to Cassadaga, too. Just don't come expecting a carnival atmosphere. Forget about gypsy women in bandannas. Don't look for signs with hands or eyes on them. You won't find them here.

The residents of Cassadaga are adamant about avoiding the pitfalls of allowing their town to become a tourist trap. It looks just like any other quaint Central Florida town, with one slight difference. Every house has a small, tasteful sign advising of the availability of services, and within those walls, instead of conventional activities, spiritual counseling, readings, and séances are being conducted.

You'll have no trouble finding someone to help with your particular problem, either. As they are quick to tell you, half the residents of Cassadaga are spiritual counselors who offer readings in their homes. The other half are long departed and have crossed into another world!

The Ann Stevens House Bed and Breakfast

The Ann Stevens House Bed and Breakfast

You'll need a place to stay when you come to visit Cassadaga, and one of the best places, no doubt, is the Ann Stevens House. One of the camp's original buildings, the Ann Stevens House has been called "the best country inn in Florida." On the National Registry of Historic Places, the bed and breakfast has a AAA Three Diamond rating and has been selected for the *Best Places to Stay* guide.

The house is located on property that was part of George Colby's original homestead. Colby sold that portion to Ann Stevens, a prominent spiritualist from Michigan. The two were good friends, and Colby was a frequent visitor to the three-story Victorian-style house that Stevens built in the 1890s.

The house changed ownership many times in the ensuing years, serving as a place of lodging at least one other time in its history. Renovations to the house include the addition of a carriage house in 1990, and an English-style pub called Sherlock's. A courtyard contains a screened Victorian-style gazebo with a hot tub, and many of the rooms include Jacuzzi tubs.

That's all well and good. But perhaps the best amenities the Ann Stevens House has to offer are its resident ghosts. Should you stay there, you might just experience one of the many mysterious incidents in recent years that have convinced the owners they have guests from another world staying here.

In one incident a woman staying in the Peaches and Cream Room was sound asleep in the comfortable queen bed. She awoke when she felt someone sit down on the bed. She then felt the covers pulled up and tucked in around her.

When Madge Clauser, owner of the bed and breakfast, heard about it, she felt sure it was the spirit of Ann Stevens. She had loved the house, and it didn't take a lot of imagination to figure out that she might return to care for it and her guests.

That theory was strengthened by another incident that occurred when the Clausers were discussing a change they wanted to make. The original section of the house has been left unchanged, and they were thinking of knocking out a wall and expanding the front of the building. As they talked, they noticed that a hanging vase with a candle in it began to sway, gently at first, but as the discussion was continued, the swaying increased, finally becoming quite violent. There was no wind in the area. No reason for the glass vase to sway like that, unless it was being pushed by unseen hands. Hands that wanted the house to be left alone. The Clausers concurred, nixing the idea of the expansion and leaving the house true to the original blueprint. The vase, they say, has been still.

In addition to these events, another guest reported hearing a child cry, "Mommy, Mommy," during the middle of one dark night. There were, however, no children staying there. There have also been reports of cold places and the feeling of a male presence when no one was there.

The mysterious incidents prompted the Clausers to allow a paranormal research group to stage an investigation in the house, in hopes of identifying the spirits who live here. The group found a large amount of energy in the house and think they identified at least one of the entities.

The closet behind the Peaches and Cream Room, where the lady guest was tucked in, was a veritable vortex of energy, the investigators said. Some of the investigators said they were strongly drawn to the closet, and others seemed to be repelled, to the point of actually feeling a push when they stepped inside.

The closet seemed to be inhabited by a male spirit, who when questioned, may have indicated that he was George Colby. However, the investigators said he seemed confused and may have been unaware of his death. As the investigators questioned this spirit, they became aware of four other spirits, including that of an older woman (Stevens, perhaps?), and a little girl.

In case you're wondering, the questioning is performed with dousing rods held in a neutral position by an investigator. The spirit supposedly uses energy to turn the rods to a "yes" or "no" position in answer to the questions. A surprising number of spirits seem quite willing to communicate in this manner.

Photographs taken throughout the Ann Stevens House revealed orbs—balls of unexplained light—mists, and rainbow images. Investigators speculated that one reason for the immense energy contained within the house may be that the house lies in a direct line with the energy vortex of Cassadaga.

Whatever the reason, the possibility of having a supernatural experience—perhaps being tucked in by Ann Stevens or being visited by Cassadaga's founder—is a great added benefit to a stay here.

Spirits of the Royalty Theater

Spirits of the Royalty Theater

Theaters are notorious for being haunted. Maybe the spirits enjoy watching the show. Maybe some of them have a bit of the ham in them. Certainly, the spirits haunting Clearwater's Royalty Theater aren't shy.

The Royalty Theater began life as the Capitol Theater, opened in 1924. It has a long and storied history, serving as a performing arts arena until the 1920s, when it became a marquee. During the World Wars, it housed both Air Force and Marine troops. In 1960, the building was almost destroyed by a storm. During the 1970s, it served a short stint as a church meeting place for youths, but was rescued in the 1980s and reincarnated as the Royalty Theater.

The new theater got off to a rocky start. In 1981, as it was being renovated for its very first production, Bill Neville, the theater's former manager, was murdered. His bound and gagged body was discovered on the theater's balcony. He had been stabbed and beaten. Police later arrested two men, both of whom were sentenced to twenty-five years in prison. They had robbed Neville of $7, they said, then had brutally slain him.

Neville, a Clearwater native, had leased the theater in 1979. Reportedly a gentle man who loved the theater, he tried for two years to revive it by featuring classic movies and occasional live entertainment. His murder was shocking to everyone.

Not long afterward, theater performers began to have strange experiences, usually at night. Sometimes voices would be heard when no one was there. And occasionally, a seat in the balcony would suddenly slam closed. The seats are quite heavy, and it's unlikely that they could close without a little help. Performers were often startled by these experiences, but they never reported feeling threatened.

The new theater struggled along for several years, but once again it failed to make a go of it. The building was closed in 1995 and soon was slated for demolition. It looked as if a large part of Clearwater's history was about to be razed.

Enter stage left: Socrates Charos. It had long been a dream of his to buy the dilapidated old building and turn it back into a theater. He seemed inexplicably drawn to the structure. When, in 1999, he followed his dream, bought the building, and started renovations, he thought he was prepared for anything—difficult workmen, bad weather, cranky decorators—anything. Wrong. It seems there was one contingency he hadn't planned for—ghosts in the theater.

Charos had heard stories, yes, but he discounted them. That is, until three weeks after renovations had begun. That's when he learned they were more than just stories. He was inside the theater alone, when he looked up to see a man standing in front of him. The fellow had a mustache and was wearing a blue coat and a fisherman's cap.

Thinking the man had just entered through the theater's west entrance, Charos greeted him and asked if he could help him. Right before his eyes, the man just disappeared, like he evaporated, Charos said. "One minute he was there. The next he wasn't."

The man has appeared to others in the theater, too. On one occasion, the construction supervisor was talking on his phone inside the theater. He thought he was alone, but when he glanced across the room, he saw a mustachioed gentleman wearing a blue coat and a cap. Before the supervisor could speak to him, the guy repeated his disappearing act. Now you see him. Now you don't.

Shaken, the supervisor rushed next door to Pat Lokey's dress shop, looking for a live body—somebody, anybody, as long as it was a breathing body. He ran into the man who lived over the shop. He excitedly asked him if he believed in ghosts. The gentleman's reply was surprising. Yes, he said, he believed in them. He, in fact, lived with one. Turns out the apparition in the cap was a wanderer. He also haunted the dress shop.

Because of the fisherman's cap the apparition wore, Charos named him the "Captain." Although he was never threatening, Charos said he had a thing for the ladies, often grabbing their legs or patting them on the rear. If he wasn't happy with something happening on stage, he would raise a horrible racket, a sound like metal pots being crashed together.

Other mysterious events occurred during the renovation. The Captain wasn't the only spirit making himself known. Often the theater lights would turn on and off for no reason—that the living could fathom, anyway—and from time to time, a decorator's book with a heavy cover would fly open. The pages would turn as if someone was looking through it, deciding on colors and patterns, no doubt. It was their home, after all. They probably felt as if they should have a say in its decoration.

In another occurrence that gave some of the workmen the heebie-jeebies, a tool that was left lying on a table suddenly started spinning in a counterclockwise direction. It stopped spinning for several seconds then started back—spinning in the opposite direction!

All these events, though startling and unexplained, have been mischievous, as if the spirits are looking to have a little fun at the expense of the living. There is one event at the theater, however, that has dark undertones, one that is quite disturbing.

The "trouble spot," as Charos calls it, is a place on a wall near the stage. On that wall is an image that resembles a knife. It's an image that refuses to go away. Charos said that even after thirty coats of paint, the image was still visible.

The Royalty Theater is a paranormal researcher's dream and, luckily, in Charos they have an owner willing to open the doors to them. One of the researchers to visit the Royalty was Paul Daniels, president of the College of Metaphysical Studies in Clearwater. He brought four faculty members with him. They were not disappointed.

All five members of the group, said Daniels, detected the presence of spirits in the theater. There are two spirits living in the balcony, one of whom calls himself William. William…Bill? Aha! A spirit lives in one of the upstairs dressing rooms, and the spirits of a woman and a child were also noted floating around.

There is one other remarkable spirit inhabiting the Royalty. Charos and others involved with the theater call her "Angelina" or "Angelica." Researchers say she is the spirit of a young woman who died in the late 1800s. A carefree spirit, she loved dance and music. Today, she freely roams the theater, often taking to the stage to dance. She's a strong presence, and Charos says he believes it was her energy that first drew him to the theater.

A devout Greek Orthodox Christian, Charos said that in the beginning, these supernatural events concerned him. After sightings of the Captain in those first weeks, he called in a priest to bless the place, and hopefully rid it of any evil spirits. The Captain has not been seen since that ceremony.

The other spirits, however, remain active. Charos said he considered calling in a priest to perform an exorcism to rid the Royalty of all her otherworldly spirits. He has since changed his mind. He believes the spirits that live there are good spirits. For whatever reason, they have chosen to move into the Royalty and live out their eternity there. He thinks they're there to look over the theater and its patrons. They are, he believes, angels.

The Ghosts of Cedar Key

The Ghosts of Cedar Key

The Island Hotel was built in 1859, in a time when folks knew how to build things to last. The builders mixed oyster shell with limestone and sand, and poured ten-inch thick walls. Massive twelve-inch oak beams framed the basement to support the wooden structure. This method of construction has withstood the ravages of nearly 150 years of hurricanes, floods, and storms. She's been battered badly at times. But she still stands.

The structure was built by Major John Parsons and Francis Hale, and was opened in 1860 as Parsons and Hale's General Store. The two hoped to cash in on the prosperity that was anticipated with the completion of the Florida Railroad. Unfortunately, that little disagreement known as the War Between the States got in the way. Cedar Key was invaded and every structure in the town was burned except the general store. It was used as a Union headquarters for a time, and most probably was used by the Confederates as well.

After the war, the general store was reopened and

Parsons and Hale finally enjoyed some of that prosperity they'd hoped for. Everything you needed for life on Cedar Key you could buy at the general store—furniture, food, hardware, fuel, oil, farm supplies and equipment, and produce. You name it; they had it. Or they could get it for you.

Parsons and Hale also were prominent in shipping and were involved in the fishing and turtle industries. Because of their shipping connections, the general store housed the customs office and the post office.

Somewhere around 1884, the store began offering accommodations and meals to travelers, most likely using the downstairs for the store and the upstairs to accommodate guests. There's a possibility, just maybe, it could be, that President Grover Cleveland might have slept there. Rumors are that the president visited Cedar Key after a visit to Cuba sometime during the early 1890s. It's reported that if he did indeed visit, there's a good possibility that he slept at Parsons and Hale's. That's not substantiated, mind you.

The bad times hit in 1896, starting with a hurricane that devastated Cedar Key and severely damaged the store. Things only worsened with the collapse of the cedar industry, which was big here on

Cedar Key. Finally, in 1910, Francis Hale died, and then in 1914, the Parsons family sold the store to Simon Feinberg.

Feinberg turned the store into the Bay Hotel, adding second-floor balconies to the southern and western sides of the building. Feinberg ran into a little trouble with his manager and died of mysterious causes in 1919.

After that, the hotel ran through many owners, many names, and many incarnations. It was called Cedar Key Hotel in the 1920s, and Fowlers Wood in the 1930s. It almost burned to the ground more than once during the Depression, when it was operated as a speakeasy and brothel. Luckily, most of the town's firefighters were customers, so each fire was quickly extinguished.

By World War II, the building had become so rundown as to be unlivable. Ah, but then the good times hit again. In 1946, Bessie and Lloyd Gibbs bought the building and restored it to its former glory. They renamed it the Island Hotel, and during their ownership, it became a notable hangout for local characters and for celebrities. On any given day, you might meet up with the likes of Tennessee Ernie Ford,

Myrna Loy, Richard Boone, and writers Pearl S. Buck and John D. McDonald.

Hurricane Easy wasn't so easy when it blew through in 1960, taking the roof with it, and requiring considerable renovations to make the building usable again. Lloyd Gibbs died in 1962, but Bessie continued to operate the hotel until 1973, when she finally had to retire for health reasons. She died two years later, when a fire burned her home in Cedar Key.

Under new ownership, the hotel underwent renovation. Then, in the early 1980s, an island troubadour named Jimmy Buffett stopped in to perform in the Neptune Lounge. He was a popular draw, and the hotel was once again a favored hangout of characters and celebrities.

The new owners continually upgrade and improve the building. However, she is an old lady, and like an old grand dame, she's settled in places. But, hey, what's a bit of sagging among friends? So what if the floors slope a bit? The rooms are nice and the food's good. What more could you ask for? Well...maybe a ghost story or two.

Would you be happy with thirteen?

That's right. Psychic investigations confirm that

the Island Hotel is quite a spiritually crowded place, with thirteen different ghosts wandering the premises. OK, so maybe we don't know the stories behind all thirteen, but we know enough. The hotel is so haunted that the Fox Network television series filmed a segment of the show *Haunted Inns and Mansions* in 1999. And every time the show airs, the hotel experiences a jump in reservations. Lots of folks out there want to see dead people. Like you. And me. For us, here are the stories behind the thirteen.

Bessie Gibbs

The psychic investigators say that former owner Bessie Gibbs's spirit is the most dominant of all the ghosts. When guests report seeing a ghostly figure moving down the hallway, they invariably describe Bessie. In life, she was a character, always full of energy. She loved to tell stories and jokes, and was ever ready to pull a prank on someone. Some things never change.

Today, Bessie wanders the hotel, rearranging furniture and straightening pictures. And closing doors. And locking them. That, it seems, is one of her favorite pranks—to lock a guest out of his room. She likes to give a good scare, too, often appearing in a room in the middle of the night, then disappearing by walking through the wall.

A séance in the hotel concluded that Bessie's room (Room 29) was extremely active supernaturally. One investigator even went so far as to opine that it was a portal to another dimension. Maybe so. Or maybe Bessie's just doing as she always did—taking care of business.

Simon Feinberg and Marcus Markham

Remember I told you about Simon Feinberg buying the general store in 1914? Well, Mr. Feinberg lived in Tallahassee, so he hired a local businessman to manage the store for him. Marcus Markham was a bit of a rounder, always looking to make an easy buck or two. But Feinberg was in Tallahassee, so what could it hurt? He'd never know.

This was the time of Prohibition, and Markham, who liked a little nip himself every now and again, decided to install a whiskey still. He could nip to his heart, er, liver's content, and sell the rest. He installed the still in the ceiling and hid it with a false ceiling. It was really pretty clever, he thought. Since it could only be accessed through the kitchen pantry, he thought he'd never be found out.

Ah, but he never counted on Mr. Feinberg's fussy thoroughness when taking care of his business. The owner discovered the still's entrance in the pantry and he hit the ceiling. He was a good Christian man. A churchgoing man who believed that liquor was evil. It led to dancing and other sinning! He couldn't have this in his establishment. He wouldn't have it! By golly, he'd put a stop to it right away.

Feinberg confronted Markham, demanding an explanation. Vexed, but unconcerned, Markham offered to pay more rent. Feinberg refused, indignantly spouting his objections to the evils of liquor. Seeing that he would not be dissuaded, Markham tried to placate his boss, telling him that, yes, of course, if he objected that strongly, he would remove the still. No. No. He wouldn't sell any more liquor. He swore. It was just a misjudgment on his part. It wouldn't happen again.

Markham suggested Feinberg go to the restaurant and calm down over a cool drink. They'd get together for dinner a little later and discuss other matters that needed to be handled.

Slightly mollified, Feinberg did as Markham

suggested. And he very much enjoyed the meal he was brought later during their meeting. He hadn't thought anything about it when Markham himself served the food and did not notice a funny taste as he ate it. No one knows, but perhaps, it did occur to Simon Feinberg to wonder about his larcenous manager's solicitousness later that night. No one knows, for the maid found him dead of poisoning in Room 27 the next morning.

Guess no one could prove anything, for there's no record of Markham ever standing trial for murder. Perhaps Feinberg got justice after all, though. Markham continued his illicit liquor business at the store, and one dark night that demon liquor proved to be his downfall.

While drinking heavily that night, Markham got into an argument with a steamboat captain. Fueled by alcohol, the argument turned into a violent fight, and Markham was stabbed. Not realizing the seriousness of his wound, he climbed into the attic of the store to get away from the ensuing brawl. He was found dead the next morning, hanging from the ladder in the pantry that led up to his still.

Psychic investigators have identified the spirits of

both Feinberg and Markham inhabiting the hotel. Feinberg, it seems, is still taking care of his business, wandering the hallways and occasionally appearing to guests, then quickly disappearing.

Markham's spirit, say the psychic investigators, haunts the place where he died. Kitchen employees report seeing the apparition of a man about five-foot-six, with dark hair and a mustache. He appears in the pantry and the kitchen area, and is reported to be a forceful entity.

The Boy in the Well

This is a sad one. Back before the Civil War, the manager of Parsons and Hale's hired a little African-American boy to sweep up and help around the store. One day, the manager saw the little boy putting something in his pocket. Thinking he was stealing something, the manager yelled, and the little boy ran out of the store. He was never seen again—at least not alive.

About a year later, workmen were doing maintenance on the basement water cistern, a 2,500-gallon cement tank. When they descended into the cistern, they discovered the skeletal remains of a child.

According to legend, the terrified little boy ran out of the store and got into the basement through the trapdoor at the back of the store. Still afraid that the manager would catch him, he saw the cistern and decided it was a good place to hide. He climbed in and drowned.

It's sad to think of the spirit of that scared little boy, still hiding out in the basement. It's dark and dank and scary down there. But psychic investigators confirm that his is, indeed, down there, probably expecting to be discovered and beaten at any moment.

Confederate Soldier

Nobody knows the story behind the spirit of the Confederate soldier who stands guard at the second-floor balcony, but he's the hotel's most sighted apparition. Every morning, just as the sun begins to rise, he appears. Wearing the uniform of a Confederate private soldier, he stands at attention just inside the doors of the balcony. He's visible for only a few seconds, but dozens of hotel guests report seeing him. He's the reason it's speculated that, in addition to being used as a Union headquarters for a time, the hotel also was used by the Confederates.

The "Lady" Upstairs

Ooh la la! Did we mention that at some point the hotel became a speakeasy and a brothel? The spirit who haunts Rooms 27 and 28 dates back to those days. She's believed to be the ghost of a prostitute who was murdered here in an undocumented incident. She's quite a friendly little thing. In the middle of the night, she will appear in one of those two rooms. She'll sit on the bed, give the occupant a sweet kiss on the cheek, then disappear in a cloud of blue smoke!

In addition to these most frequently seen apparitions, psychic investigators report the presence of seven other spirits who inhabit the Island Hotel. These ghosts include two Native Americans, a fisherman, and an unidentified tall, thin man.

Staying at the Island Hotel on Cedar Key obviously can be a haunting experience. If you like being kissed by strange, ethereal women, I suggest you request Room 27 or Room 28. I'm thinking you might want to avoid Room 29, though, unless you're looking for an opportunity to explore another dimension!

The Pirate's Lady Loses Her Head

The Pirate's Lady Loses Her Head

"Alright, maties. Hold your own 'til they draw a mite closer." The pirate Jose Gaspar lay prone on the deck of his ship, his sword hidden beneath him. His band of cutthroats were similarly positioned, some prone, some supine, some sitting slumped over. For all the world, it looked as if they were a ship met with violence and let adrift. Gaspar knew the captain of the Spanish galleon would not be able to resist checking it out.

He stole a glance at the ship. She was beautiful and stately, her sails billowing in the wind. And he hated her. That is, he hated the country she sailed from. His country once. But no more.

He almost laughed out loud, remembering his last day in the land of his birth. An admiral in high standing in Spain's navy, he'd also enjoyed high favor in the king's court. Oh, yes, he could be quite courtly and polished when he wished. And the court life had suited him, the sumptuousness of it all—the rich clothes, the high favor, and the warm and willing ladies.

He'd coveted that wealth of those around him, a

wealth he didn't share. Yes, his exploits in the navy had won him favor here, but that wouldn't last. The only thing that lasted was real wealth. He felt as if he deserved some of that wealth for his service to his country and his king. So really, when he'd stolen the crown jewels, he was just taking his due. He never planned to get caught. Ah, but he'd been betrayed by that little lovely he'd bedded. He'd known she'd be his downfall when he'd been seduced by her lovely wicked eyes.

He'd only just escaped, leaping from her bed and fighting his way through the streets to the docks. He jumped aboard his ship, the prize vessel of the Spanish fleet, and ordered his men to get her underway. The soldiers, unaware of the situation, had followed orders, and they'd sailed out of the harbor without being caught, leaving behind their country and their families forever. Those soldiers now formed the core of his band of pirates.

Not long after, word had come that the king had declared a price on his head, a fact that greatly angered him. Ha! To think the king's navy could catch the great Gaspar! Just the thought of the price on his head made him hate. He had a deep hatred for all things Spanish now. And he planned to show them. He'd destroy Spain. He'd capture her ships, heavy with New World treasure. He'd shut down her commerce lines. Take her finest ships. And just where would the king and all his wealth be then? Kissing the feet of the great Gasparilla, that's where!

Another glance told him that the Spanish captain had fallen for the trick. He had come about and was dropping his sails. "Steady, men," he whispered. "They're comin' for it."

The men held their positions, still as the dead they were pretending to be until the full contingent of the Spanish ship had boarded. Then they sprang to life, attacking and killing the boarding party in short order. Some of Gaspar's men jumped the small gap to the deck of the other ship, carrying lines with them. They lashed the two ships together, rendering the ship's cannons unusable.

Gaspar fought with relish, laughing each time he ran his sword into the flesh of his enemy. Soaked in their blood, he slashed his way aboard the other ship and searched for their captain. There he was, the coward, standing up there atop the poop deck, looking down on the action.

"Avast thar, matey," Gaspar called above the noise of the melee. "Aren't you going to come down and fight me?"

The captain only stared. There was a look of fear, but there was defiance, too.

"Come on down, me hearty. I'll give you a chance." Gaspar swung his sword in a challenge.

The captain stayed up on his roost, immobile. But it didn't matter—the bloody fight was over. The ship, its passengers, and all its treasure were now his.

"Bring me the captain!" Gaspar shouted to his men. The man was brought, bound, and thrown at his feet. "There you are, coward. Your ship is mine. How say you? How shall you die? By the sword? Or do you prefer to swim with the sharks?"

"I'll take the sword, you scoundrel."

Gaspar drew his sword. "Ah, yes, an honorable death." He raised his arm to severe the captain's head from his body, but before he could swing, he was suddenly attacked by a blur of black hair, feet, and red fingernails. He was kicked soundly as he felt the rake of the nails across his cheek, and saw them coming at him again. He grabbed the arm and tossed the wildcat away from him.

Bemused, he looked down at the spitfire. Why! It was a woman! A comely one, too, if he judged by her shape and that head of wild black hair that was hiding her face. She was dressed in Spanish finery. Her tiny feet, the ones that had just almost emasculated him, were encased in jeweled slippers, and there was a fortune in jewels on her fingers.

When she raised her face, impatiently brushing back her hair, he almost gasped. She was the most beautiful woman he'd ever seen, and he'd seen plenty. A smile crept onto his face. Ah, such treasures this ship doth hold!

Her eyes were spitting fire at him, and she was about to rise when the captain spoke.

"Princess Useppa, do not involve yourself. My fate cannot be changed."

What's this? I've netted meself a princess, thought Gaspar. This just gets better! He looked her over again. What sweet revenge, to have captured such a prize! Forget ransom, though. He was keeping this one. He had no doubt she'd heat up his bed quite nicely.

"Your captain speaks true, m'lady," said Gaspar. "'Tis the way of the sea."

She looked up at him, her eyes defiant. "It doesn't

have to be that way. You can spare him and the rest of our crew."

"Nay, princess. A pirate's only bounty is the respect of his crew. It must be done. Rodrigo!" Gaspar called to his first mate. "Take the princess to the ship and put her in my cabin. You'll be comfortable there, m'lady. Let her get some of her things, Roddy, me mate. You know how women are about their things."

He ignored the surprised look of his first mate. Normally, he never gave quarter to any captive, no matter how comely. But something in her fiery eyes had captured him. He wanted this one warm and willing when she came to his bed. So what did it matter if he allowed her to bring her things?

"Go!" He roared and turned back to the business at hand.

Rodrigo grabbed the woman by her wrist and pulled her to her feet. Ignoring her protests, he pulled her toward the cabins and summoned a couple of men to follow. No doubt, she had plenty of "things." Old Gasparilla must be gettin' daft. Caterin' to a woman!

Several hours passed before Gaspar returned to his cabin. He opened the door cautiously, expecting perhaps an attack, and stepped inside. It looked as if her valise had exploded. There were all manner of frilly things hanging everywhere. The cramped cabin had a sweet, floral smell. He breathed it in. Ah! He loved women. They'd be the death of him someday, no doubt. He'd give this one a favored spot. If she calmed down and cooperated, he could see her as his number one choice of all the women held on the island he called Captiva.

Looking around the room, he found her curled up in the cabin's small chair. She was watching him with wary eyes. He smiled and turned to the table, where the remains of her repast sat. Looked as if she still had an appetite.

"Good evening, m'lady. I see you've had your dinner. Perhaps a bit of sherry to cleanse the palate?" He poured them both a drink in the dainty glasses from some plundered ship. When he offered it to her, she slapped it from his hand. He laughed.

"You are a scoundrel, sir! A blackguard and a scoundrel! I know who you are. I know you absconded with my family's crown jewels. There's a price on your head. You'd better release me now! My father will send navies out to get me. Release me and my ship's crew now if you want to live."

He smiled sadly at her.

"I'm sorry, princess. But that's not possible. There is no longer a crew, and your ship is now mine, along with all its booty."

"No crew? You killed them all?"

"All who didn't agree to join my band."

"You wretched creature!" she slapped him soundly, and he grabbed her wrist.

Putting his face into hers, he said darkly, "I have given you more quarter than any of my captives because of your beauty and your station. But do not try me further." He released her roughly, and she stumbled back into the chair.

He poured her another drink, and she took it, her eyes finally registering fear.

"Do not look at me so, princess. I may be a blackguard and a scoundrel, as you say, but I have never taken a woman against her will. You are safe here. You'll come to me willingly one day. You'll see."

"Never!"

He just laughed. "I like a woman with fire!"

Months passed. Gaspar moved the Princess Useppa into his own quarters. He catered to her, having a cot brought in and hanging curtains to give her privacy. He'd been patient, hoping her anger at him and her situation would gradually dissipate. He'd brought her treasures of untold wealth from his plunderings—gold, jewels, dresses of the finest silk. She only looked at them and asked just what she was to do with them, stuck on this godforsaken island.

Though she treated him with an imperious attitude, she was friendly with others on the island, especially the children, with whom she exhibited a quiet gentleness, sometimes even playfulness. Watching her with them made his desire to have her ever stronger, but she spurned his every advance.

As his frustration with her grew, so did his obsession. He could think of nothing else. Her eyes, her hair, her beautiful face—they constantly occupied his mind. Why, just minutes ago, he'd been running his sword through some brigand, and suddenly the image of her smiling down at a child had popped up and he'd had to shake his head to dislodge it. It had shocked and angered him.

All his other women had lost their appeal to him, and they were angry at his lack of attention. His crew, he knew, thought him addlepated. By the gods, he was beginning to think so, too! He had to end the torment before his crew lost all respect for him. Mutiny would surely follow.

"Princess!" Gaspar entered his island quarters in full rant. "Princess! Where are you, woman!"

Hearing a sound behind him, he turned to find her standing there, eyes wide.

"What is it?"

"What is it? What is it, you ask? It's you! You're a torment to me. Day and night. It's you my addled brain dwells on! It's your face! Those eyes! I see them awake or asleep. You've cursed me, wench!"

"Nay. 'Tis not I who did the cursing. 'Tis your wickedness that's cursed you."

"Wickedness? M'lady, have I not been ever the gentleman? I have acted as a besotted swain, bringing you riches to warm the heart of any woman."

"'Tis not riches I wish, sir."

"Then, what, m'lady!" he roared, grabbing her wrist and pulling her roughly to him. "What will bring you to me willingly?"

He was enraged. Gaspar had never been a patient man. Yet he'd bided his time, believing completely in his ability to coax her into his bed. Fool! She'd rejected him time and again. He was losing the respect of his men. He was losing his self-respect. He was losing his mind!

"Tell me! What will it take?"

She spat in his face. His rage was answered in her eyes. She tried to wrench away from him. "Nothing!" She screamed. "Nothing you could ever say or do would make me submit to you!"

Twisting from his grip, she swung away and grabbed a knife from the table. Her face contorted in white-hot fury, she darted back and slashed him across the face. He howled with rage. She backed off, but when he looked up, she was coming at him again. This time the knife was raised and was aimed straight for his heart.

Gaspar the Pirate reacted. He did what he'd done countless times before in the face of a threat. He drew his sword and, without a thought, severed the princess's head from her body.

The sword hit the floor a split second after Useppa's head. Her body collapsed and Gaspar followed. He sat stunned as blood pooled around him. What had he done? It had been a reaction. Something done without thought. Now she was gone. Remorse and grief filled him. He'd never again see her touch the face of a child. Never see those beautiful eyes aimed at him in fury. What had he done?

Gaspar's grief was deep over the loss of Useppa. After her body was prepared by the women of the island, he gently placed her in a dinghy and rowed alone to the small nearby island where he had once taken her on an outing she had enjoyed. Digging the grave himself, he laid her to rest there among the palm trees filled with tropical birds. He named the island Useppa, after the beautiful Spanish princess.

According to legend, Gaspar lived and plundered for years after the death of Useppa. His death was as colorful as his life. Seems that in 1821, he had decided to retire from his life of pillaging and go straight. He had amassed a fortune, all of it buried on what is now Gasparilla Island. He now had the wealth he needed to buy himself a life of respectability.

His crew, however wanted to attack one more ship. They had spotted it, a fat British merchant ship, sailing into Charlotte Harbor. Defenseless, it would be easy pickings.

When Gasparilla and his crew attacked, they

quickly learned that the ship was instead the pirate-hunting American ship the USS *Enterprise*. The battle was fierce, but when it was obvious the cause was lost, Gaspar—who liked to call himself Gasparilla—vowed never to be taken. Tying the anchor around himself, he leapt into the briny deep.

Every year in January, Tampa is overrun by pirates during the annual Pirate Fest, which celebrates the legend of Gasparilla. These are, of course, only local residents playing dress up. They ignore the nasty rumor that Gasparilla and his exploits were the figment of the imaginations of a group of Charlotte Harbor land developers. If that rumor's true, it was quite a successful ploy, for the story of Gasparilla is a popular one and most believe it to be true.

Whether or not Jose Gaspar truly existed doesn't really matter. Real pirates did, indeed, sail the Florida waters and utilize Captiva Island, where Gasparilla reportedly kept his female captives; Gasparilla Island, which he used as his headquarters and where he may have buried his treasure; and Useppa Island, the story of which you now know.

Many believe that pirates of the Gulf are sailing

these waters still. There have been sightings of ghostly images along the coasts of these islands. Other pirate spirits have been sighted on the small island of Cayo Pelau. They are, it's said, the spirits of Gasparilla's crew. Cayo Pelau was their island and it's where they buried their share of the booty. On dark nights, they can be seen roaming the island, still protecting their treasure.

Perhaps the most interesting—and frightening—spirit haunts Useppa Island. When development of the island began many years ago, excavations uncovered a human skeleton. There was something different about this skeleton—it was obvious from markings on the bones that its head had been severed from the body.

The inn now known as Gasparilla Cottage was built on this site in 1914, and it's here that guests have reported sighting the ghost of a headless woman roaming the grounds.

Two hundred years ago, the Gulf waters teemed with the ships of pirates, who used the Florida coast and nearby islands as a base of operations. They lived and loved here. And when then died, they left millions of dollars in gold, jewels, and other treasures buried beneath the sands. Is it any wonder that their spirits still patrol these waters?

The Ghost Bride of the Casa De La Paz

The Ghost Bride of the Casa De La Paz

Go ahead and pack up, honey," said the young groom. "Our train doesn't leave until 4:00. I'll be back way before that time."

"But it's our last day here!" His bride lamented. "What'll I do all day while you're off fishing?"

"Once you finish packing, you can go shopping. Here," he fished out his wallet and handed her a wad of bills. "Go pick up that lamp you liked so much. It's just the thing for our new great room."

Taking the money, she smiled. The lamp would be perfect for their new house in Boston, and he had been loathe to spend the money yesterday. If allowing a few hours fishing out on the bay would get it for her, why fuss?

She kissed him. "OK. But don't you be late. And be careful! I don't want anything happening to my new husband!"

"Nothing will happen, dear. It's a beautiful sunny day. I'll be back in plenty of time to clean up and be ready to leave."

After he left, the young woman began packing, lovingly placing his clothes into the valise. She was so happy! She loved her new husband so much. He was tall and handsome and so loving.

June 23, 1917, had been the most wonderful day of her life—her wedding day. And they'd left that evening for their honeymoon trip down to St. Augustine. It was really nice of her father's friend, Mr. Puller, to allow them to stay in his beautiful home while he and his family were away. If he hadn't been so generous, they'd never have been able to afford such a wonderful trip. And it had been truly glorious! She was sorry to see it end. But then she was looking forward to getting back to their new house to start her life as a married woman, too.

Finished packing, she quickly bathed and dressed and headed out for the little shops just up the street from the house. She remembered just which one she had seen that lamp in. It was a Tiffany lamp, with just the right colors in it. It wasn't very large either, so it wouldn't be difficult to get it back on the train.

As she stepped from the shop with her package, a sudden wind ruffled her hair. It felt different, cooler than when she entered the shop. Looking around, she saw that the sky out over the bay had darkened dramatically. A niggle of worry started in her stomach, but she pushed it away. It was time for her husband to be back. There was no need to worry about a storm brewing.

She hurried back to the house. He'd be here anytime. As she unlocked the door to enter, she turned for another glance over the water. A brilliant jagged bolt of lightning split the dark sky, and clouds of rain obscured sight of the water. It looked like a really bad storm, and it had blown up so fast.

Praying that her husband was already docked safe and sound, she ran upstairs and began wrangling the suitcases downstairs. Might as well be ready to go when he got there. She piled everything in the parlor and sat down in a chair, the lamp in her lap and suitcases surrounding her. He would be here any minute. She was sure.

The Pullers found her there when they returned two days later. She still sat in the chair amid all the luggage, the lamp clutched tightly to her. Her face was tear-stained, and she was rocking back and forth.

"It's time to go. We're going to miss the train." She looked up at the Pullers when they entered, bewilderment in her eyes. "The train will be leaving soon. He has to get cleaned up and dressed. It's time to go."

The young bride's husband, of course, did not return. His boat was lost at sea during a sudden violent thunderstorm, and his body was never found. His bride reportedly was so grief stricken that she could not bear to leave. She stayed in St. Augustine, pining away for her handsome husband and the happy life they had planned together. She was often seen walking along the beach, looking worriedly out to sea, as if he'd left just that morning and would be returning momentarily.

According to legend, the bride died a few years later—of a broken heart no doubt—but though her earthly body is gone, her spirit remains. Legend says she's stayed in her honeymoon house through its many incarnations, still awaiting the return of her husband.

The house was once converted to apartments, and this was when sightings of the young bride were first reported. Tenants reported hearing a knock at their door and a plaintive voice asking, "Is it time to leave yet?"

The sightings have continued since the home was

turned into a bed and breakfast. Sometimes it's the knock on the door followed by the questions. Other times, it's the sound of a door closing and the glimpse of a figure walking down the hall. Sometimes the bride is seen, sitting among all her luggage, still waiting for her husband to come so they can begin living happily ever after.

About the Author

Lynne L. Hall is a native Southerner who is well acquainted with the people and places that make these stories so interesting to read and share. Her work has appeared in *Cosmopolitan*, *Penthouse*, *Popular Science*, *Physical*, and in many other magazines. She is the author of the Strange But True series of books that includes volumes on Alabama, Florida, Georgia, Virginia, and Tennessee.

Other ghostly tales from Lynne's pen are found in *Tennessee Ghosts*, *North Carolina Ghosts*, and *South Carolina Ghosts*.